REDUCE!

211 Strategies To Reduce Your Real Estate Cost

Wayne Fox

Copyright © 2015 by Wayne Fox. All rights reserved. No part of this book may be reproduced in any form without permission in writing from the author.
Reviewers may quote brief passages in reviews.

Disclaimer and FTC Disclaimer

No part of this publication may be reproduced or transmitted in any form or by any means, mechanical or electronic, including photocopying or recording, or by any information storage and retrieval system, or transmitted by email without permission in writing from the publisher.

While all attempts have been made to verify the information provided in this publication, the author does not assume any responsibility for errors, omissions, or contrary interpretations of the subject matter herein.

This book is for entertainment purposes only. The views expressed are those of the author alone, and should not be taken as expert instruction or commands. The reader is responsible for his or her own actions.

Adherence to all applicable laws and regulations, including international federal, state, and local governing professional licensing, business practices, advertising, and all other aspects of doing business in the US, Canada, UK, or any other jurisdiction is the sole responsibility of the purchaser or reader.

The author does not assume any responsibility or liability whatsoever on the behalf of the purchaser or reader of this material.

Any perceived slight of any individual or organization is purely unintentional. I sometimes use affiliate links with the content of the book. This means by making a purchase, I will get a sales commission. This, however, does not mean my opinion is for sale. Any affiliate links listed in the book are the services and products for which I've used myself and found useful. The reader or purchaser should do their own research before making a purchase online.

Contents

1. Introduction
2. PART 1: Real Estate
3. PART 2: Maintaining Your Property
4. PART 3: Energy
5. Conclusion
6. About the Author

Introduction

Real Estate can make up a significant portion of costs faced by a business. Many small business owners are too busy to start learning how they might reduce their costs, so we have compiled a simple, easy to read guide listing some core strategies to reduce real estate costs and make a small business more profitable.

This eBook is primarily focused on small business premises, but the same principles can be copied for all real estate types, from the family home to large manufacturing plants the size of a small city.

For ease of reading, this book is split into 3 parts:
- Part 1 - Real Estate – The core building structure, and everything associated with that
- Part 2 - Maintaining the premises – The process of keeping the systems running efficiently
- Part 3 - Energy – The process of reducing the cost of energy to the business

This eBook is written mostly from the point of long term strategy, whilst some strategies have an immediate payoff, other strategies have a longer term payoff with some investment needed upfront. It is advisable to calculate the payback of any strategy covered in the book, to verify its suitability in your own circumstances.

PART 1: Real Estate

Since we're all busy people, let's jump right in and get on with it, starting with our Real Estate section. This will cover everything related to the core building structure.

1. **Get the best deal from the start.**
   When looking for real estate, negotiate a deal that's right for your business. Most leases are set up to benefit the landlord. We'll look at more ways to do this later.

2. **Optimize opening times according to levels of trade.**

   If your business is open at 9 am, but you only get a couple of customers for the first two hours, is it costing you more to pay for staff and running costs than the profit you make from those sales? If the sales presence is needed, could the resource requirement be reduced in some way to accommodate the reduced footfall?

3. **Use double/triple shift patterns for the building.**

   Most buildings are only used for eight to ten hours a day. What other uses could you find for your space outside of those core opening times? One example could be an office building. By changing the building's occupancy to a double shift system, the 8 am-6 pm workforce go home at 6 pm, and a new workforce of staff work between 7 pm and 7 am.

These daytime staff could be the customer facing staff, and the night shift staff could be the people performing tasks such as payroll and accounts, which do not need to be customer facing. This not only reduces seat numbers for the business, but also increases profitability. For a business working eight hours a day, this could be further optimized by having three shift patterns. What could your business do with its space after hours?

4. **Consider the location for your business.**
If your business doesn't need to be in the prime city center, it can be significantly cheaper, in capital purchase cost, rent, and government taxes, to get a building that's a few streets away, or more radically, on the outskirts of town.

5. **Position your business where your customers are.**

   Looking at footfall to the business, positioning your premises central to where your customers are might not reduce initial property costs, but it will reduce wastage costs for staff who aren't fully effective as they don't have enough customers to keep them busy.

6. **Get the right type of property.**

   Do you really need retail space or could you work from an office building? Retail space is typically the most expensive space to rent or buy, and often carries the highest cost for both rental and government taxes.

   Warehousing per square feet is around the least expensive type of property. Understanding and optimizing how your business operates could significantly reduce costs.

Understanding the future of your industry and setting up your business in that way will also save you money in the longer term.

For example, if you're a retail business, can you predict the future of how people will shop?

Some experts would say that more shopping will be done online in the future. If this is the case, then moving a large part of your operations into warehousing space and reducing the retail space would be a wise move in terms of reducing cost and positioning the business for future trends in the industry.

7. **Reduce travel time for staff.**

   If your business has a requirement for staff to visit customers away from your premises, consider the cost of travelling time from your premises to the customer. If your premises are based on the outskirts of the city, but your customers are in the city center, you'll be paying them, perhaps half an hour travelling each way every time they make that journey. That's one hour of wasted productivity for every visit to a customer.

8. **Reduce travel expenses for staff.**

   As with travel time for staff, if you're paying for travel expenses to visit customers, it could get very costly for your business in paying for fuel, vehicles, train tickets, etc.

9. **Map where your customers are.**

    By taking a large geographic map of the area, and plotting where your customers are located, you can build up a heat map of where your largest audience is, and base your premises close to that. If you find your customers are spread between three main locations, you may find it cheaper to have three smaller separate premises rather than one central building.

    Consider total costs in this assessment, as sometimes small premises carry reduced or zero government taxes, whilst having three separate locations may cost more in managing them.

10. **Consider hot-desking.**

    Hot-desking has been around since around 2009. Instead of giving a staff member a permanent desk space, you give them temporary access to a desk space with all the facilities they need while they are onsite. This works well for positions such as salespeople who spend a lot of time away from the office.

There are also many different office space providers that provide hot-desking space, so rather than renting a full office space, you can simply pay by the hour. This can be good especially if you or your staff may be working a good distance away from your office and you don't want to pay them to travel to your premises.

The concept can be copied for most industries where permanent space isn't required.

11. Adopt a remote working policy.

Remote working is being used by many of the large businesses. Rather than paying for space to house staff, they work remotely either from home or from their vehicles, some incorporating an element of hot-desking in other people's buildings. Adopting remote working can reduce the need for space significantly.

12. Use shared space.

A more common example of this is renting space within a business center. The same model can be copied across most industries, however.

For example, if you're a retailer, you can share space with other retailers, perhaps even with larger brands on the high street. Your objective is to sell your product/service to the customer, it isn't to rent or own a building; that's a completely different industry.

13. Calculate the balance ratio between shared space and dedicated space.

By understanding what the break point is between buying shared space and buying your own dedicated space, you know when the most efficient time is to look for your own premises.

For example, on making a quick search for both types of property, we found a business center space which rented for $300/mn per seat. In searching for rented office space, we found an 1100 sq. ft. property which would seat between 11-15 seats. This was $1,900 rent per month including all government taxes. Both buildings had utilities additional so we haven't considered these costs in this example. By running these numbers, we can see that the breakpoint is around 7 seats.

Obviously you also have to weigh up the cost of fitting out a building; business centers usually come already fitted out, and include desks, IT and power outlets. All of these fit out costs should be factored into your equation though these can be spread over a long period of time.

14. Negotiate a longer term rent period.

Agreeing to a longer term lease period can help reduce your monthly rental cost as landlords will often favor having the guarantee of a long term tenant as it reduces the cost to them of marketing vacant premises.

15. Look for incentives when negotiating a rental agreement.

This goes for both rented and shared space. The landlord will often be willing to offer incentives such as free rent periods or added value services such as free meeting rooms if renting in a shared space building. Occasionally when premises are built in large numbers, the landlord will build them without having a tenant in mind, so talking to landlords with new developments especially during the construction phase can lead to favorable terms.

They may also be able to make introductions to potential customers. After all, it's in their interest for your business to be successful. It's worth asking the question.

16. Have the best security measures.

Although it may seem like a cost to the business, not having it could give the business a significant cost later on down the line, which could even mean complete business failure.

17. Don't occupy more space than you need.

This will reduce rent, rates, maintenance, heating & cooling. I meet so many business owners that take on a lot more space than they need, and wind up using the excess space for storage. If you need storage space, there are much cheaper options available.

18. Sublet any surplus space.

Subject to gaining agreement from the landlord, why not partner with other business owners, and sublet space to them? If it's a complementary business, it might even add some value to both businesses by working together in such a way.

19. Look at other uses for your space.

Assessing how your business operates, and what its customers' buying habits are, could free up space to be used more effectively.

For example, a café might find that 75% of its sales are takeaway, thus cutting down its required seating space; it could use that space for anything from subletting office space for business meetings to starting a complimentary baking business. It doesn't matter what you use the extra space for (subject to licensing), but just have this strategy in mind for your own premises.

20. **Don't pay more rent than you need to.**
A professional advisor will advise you of the current market rents, and where a property is overpriced. They will also help negotiate any incentives.

21. **Don't pay what the premises are marketed at.**
Just because the premises are marketed at $10,000 a month doesn't mean the agent or landlord expects to get $10,000 a month.

As with everything in life and business, negotiation is key, and starting low with offers can only benefit you. The worst that can happen is that they'll refuse the offer, and you'll have to make a higher one.

22. Don't use a lawyer to make informal offers on premises.

Instead of having a lawyer draw up various legal documents stating informal offers for either capital purchases or leases, just use the telephone and email until a figure and basic terms have been agreed upon. Then have the landlord's agent send through the documents for signing. This way you're only paying for having the documents checked over rather than writing them from scratch.

23. Buy the premises rather than lease it.

Weighing up the mortgage cost against the leasing cost can help in some cases, reducing the monthly outgoings for the business in leasing premises. In doing so, obviously be sure the business isn't going to outgrow the premises too quickly, and the property makes a good investment in terms of resale potential later on.

Have your accountant run through the numbers, including any tax incentives for both the ownership and rental options.

24. Release capital in an owned property using a sale and lease back process.

Many banks and financial institutions offer a way for commercial real estate owners to free up their asset value by selling it to the bank and then leasing it back on fixed terms.

As with strategy 23, talk this through with your accountant to assess the implications on the business, as a large capital gain achieved on the real estate could lead to a very large tax bill, meaning the option is less viable.

25. **If buying real estate, consider buying from auction.**

    Buying at auction can provide a good opportunity to get a bargain on commercial premises. Many large commercial portfolios are owned by Real Estate trusts, insurance companies and mutual funds, and so they sell off large portions of their portfolio in one go. This means it presents a good opportunity for anyone looking for commercial premises.

    Before bidding at auction on any property, it is advisable to seek assistance from experienced advisors and also ensure you have the capital lined up to complete the purchase within a few days of the hammer falling.

In many jurisdictions you will be required to pay a fairly large deposit on the day of the auction, and failure to pay within the agreed timescale will mean you incurring very large fines.

26. Convert a building to your needs.

By converting an existing building, changing its use (subject to consent) could give you an amazing opportunity to save money on both lease costs and purchase costs. For example, converting part of a warehousing space into office space would save substantial rent over the alternative of taking the equivalent office space elsewhere.

Obviously you will need to consider zoning restrictions, as the planning or licensing authorities probably wouldn't agree to you converting an entire warehouse into an office premises, though they probably would agree to converting a portion of the premises.

27. Understand the landlord's agenda.

Do they want income now, or security in the future? Structure the lease around that agenda.

28. Consider joint partnership with the landlord.

If real estate is a major factor in the business success and growth of your business, (supermarkets being a prime example) consider requesting the landlord accept a share of profits/equity in the business in exchange for a large reduction in rent.

The landlord would need to have an enterprising nature to accept this, but there are a few major property landlords who structure this type of arrangement.

29. Check to ensure that your business rateable value is correct.

Business premise taxes are, in some jurisdictions, calculated based on the value of the real estate. This value can be disputed. Using an expert to challenge this can help you achieve a result.

30. Apply for small business exemption for both water and business rates.

Organizations with charitable status can normally get either complete exemption or part exemption, and some small businesses will also qualify for exemptions. Regions vary, and can depend on local industries.

31. Have a water rate liability audit and challenge any taxes on water.

Having an audit will identify if water rate liability is high. Some authorities charge on either, a per usage charge, or a fixed charge. Calculating the best option based on your usage levels will help you reduce the cost.

32. Understand your service charge and what is included.

Your service charge can include any number of things from supplying you with reception services to cleaning and coffee making facilities, right down to cleaning or if you're lucky, free access to the onsite gym facilities. By having this broken down, it gives you a clearer picture about what you might be paying for twice, or even what you can probably do without.

33. Negotiate a service charge reduction.

Negotiate for a reduction of service charge where services are not needed or where the service charge doesn't offer the best value for each service being provided.

For example, they may offer call answering services which cost twice as much as using an outsourced call handling firm. If you only take one or two calls per week, why not just have it diverted to your mobile phone?

34. Convert a building only after assessing life cycle costs.

If converting an existing building to change its use, assess the life cycle and conversion costs against that of a building which is already designed for that purpose.

It's important to understand how many years it will take to recoup that conversion cost. Taking into the consideration the market resale value for the newly converted building too.

35. **Avoid problems to reduce any professional fees.**

    Opting not to cause a reason for argument with the landlord or neighboring businesses will remove any need to instruct professional advisors such as lawyers. Properly maintaining a building will also prevent interference from the landlord or their agent.

36. Reduce tax liability on property by choosing the correct structure.

One option could be to set up a legal entity for the sole purpose of owning the property, then lease it to the business, thus keeping the core business separate from the tax liabilities incurred from owning the property.

37. Consider refinancing if a property is owned.

A good finance broker can advise you on when is a good time to refinance. Such a move could also release additional built up equity from any value increases. It's important to be aware of the tax implications when doing this.

38. Consolidate remote operations.

If operating from more than one site, consider consolidating some of the operations to gain efficiencies.

You could thus possibly increase the size of one property while significantly reducing the size of other properties. The cost per sqft of space is often cheaper for a larger building than a smaller building.

39. Outsource 'non-core functions' to reduce demand for space.

If your business is a restaurant, the core function of the business is to provide food to customers. If you have to employ staff to do anything other than prepare and serve the food, these are considered non-core functions, and they can distract the business from providing its service.

Such non-core functions could include staff recruitment, payroll, accounts, marketing, table reservations, property management, cleaning, call answering, etc.

In larger buildings, there may well be a need for a full time presence for some of these functions, such as a cleaner, but outsourcing this role removes the need to manage that role or individual.

Such management or supervision will distract the business and its staff from serving its customers and, dependent on the function, could need a level of training or expertise by the business managers in order to manage that function properly.

40. **Share demand for products, services and space with others around you**.
Coming together with similar businesses can help reduce the cost of particular products or services. For example, consider the latest high rise property developments being built over the last couple of years.

Rather than a building being built by one company, for example, a hotel, it's now much more common to build a larger building, and divide it up into hotel space, office space, gym space, residential space, restaurant space, and even retail space.

We don't need to look at the 110 floor high rise buildings to see examples of this; we can see it in most new developments in any city. It might only be 6 or 8 stories high, but it'll still encompass hotel space, retail space on the ground floor, and offices on the remainder space.

By doing this, these building occupants get the benefits of being in such a location together with the other businesses, but can share the cost of the building such as maintaining the grounds, security, IT infrastructure, reception desk services, cleaning, facilities management, right down to bulk buying of their toilet rolls for the building, simply by adding an extra floor, or extending the floor area slightly.

41. **Share critical systems with similar businesses.**

Putting in place critical systems and infrastructure can be extremely expensive for any business operating individually. By working with other businesses, each can benefit from the core back bone of the systems, with each just having a much smaller cost for personal tailoring of the systems.

A good example of this can be seen with 'cloud storage'. Just a few years ago, a company would have to invest in its own IT servers, & its own custom software. Running a business was costly.

When cloud services came online, the core backbone was provided remotely while each business just set up the service according to their own operating needs. There is still efficiency to be gained by further grouping this demand together.

42. Collate property supplies with other buyers.

Collating the demand for property supplies means that rather than buying 20 toilet rolls a month, the combined buying power might be 20,000 toilet rolls a month. This means you can gain sufficient buying power to negotiate directly with the manufacturer rather than buying retail, or even wholesale.

This is effectively how the wholesale market works. Its customers are a group of similar businesses, and as such, they can negotiate greater discounts according to the buying habits of its customers.

43. **Collate space requirements.**

Coming together with others opens up an avenue to share space with them. For example let's imagine there are five local businesses, three have a need for short term space, while the other two have space available due to fostering a new remote working plan for its staff. There is also a local community center that has office space available but it is hardly ever used.

By coming together, all of this space can be utilized as if it were one large business, with each just paying/being paid for the space being utilized while each achieves maximum space utilization.

44. **Employ a good real estate lawyer.**

A good property lawyer will test the lease for 'reasonableness' and can fight for a fairer tenant biased and friendlier lease.

45. Reduce insurance premiums by increasing excess.

Increasing the excess on any policy can reduce insurance premiums, especially in higher risk or newer businesses.

46. Don't over value for insurance.

Get an up to date valuation to avoid over valuing and critically under valuing.

47. Insure only for rebuilding.

When buying buildings insurance, you only need to insure for the cost of re-building, which should be much less than the actual market value.

48. Pay your insurance premium upfront.

Check with your insurer if it's possible to save money by paying upfront, and if cash flow will allow it, do so.

Ensure in doing so that if you need to make alterations to the policy later on, that you won't be hit with extra costs.

49. Avoid increasingly higher insurance costs, try to avoid claiming if possible.

Increasing the excess can deter making a claim for insignificant amounts, as the cost of repairs will likely be substantially less than the excess.

50. Scan all paperwork to the cloud.

Rather than storing box files full of old invoices and expense reports, scan them all into your cloud storage, getting rid of all the paper copies, and saving on storage costs. To save on this further, rather than scanning the documents and storing them in your main company cloud drive, why not use one the free cloud services, then share access to the drive with anyone in the company that might need it

PART 2:

Maintaining Your Property

51. **Reduce dilapidation costs to the real estate.**
    This can be achieved by having a preventive maintenance program in place for all building services and building fabric.

52. **Keep your property in a good state of repair.**

Under a lease agreement, and under the health and safety regulations, it is your responsibility to properly maintain your premises. A planned and preventive maintenance plan can be performed at minimal costs to the business. It also represents a much better image to customers and staff.

Landlords as well as government authorities have the right to issue an interim schedule of repair, along with potential fines.

In the event of injuries, penalties can also include custodial sentences for the business owner and the management team. Insurance companies also insist on keeping the building properly maintained, and will refuse a claim if it doesn't have documented evidence of maintenance being carried out, and a current plan of maintenance in place.

53. **Use software to control property maintenance issues.**

    Using a professional software package to report, track and manage any maintenance issues frees up your memory to focus on running your business rather than monitoring when a contractor will arrive to fix any problems. There are a number of free or low cost packages available now.

54. **Use an asset register with a history log.**

    By using an asset register with a documented history log, you can record the history of items and identify how the item has been maintained, when it was last inspected, and when the item was last replaced.

A good history log should also let you link certain documents to the items too, such as contractor invoices, or copies of warranty certificates

55. Collate demand for property services with other businesses.

To reduce administrative and management costs, many service providers will often only focus on larger customers. This is because it takes the same resources to manage and invoice a customer with one property as it does a customer with 50 properties.

If they have to manage 50 customers individually, that's 50 points of contact, 50 contracts, 50 tenders, 50 purchase orders, 50 invoices, etc. By coming together with others, the contractor is motivated to provide services cheaper as they have reduced administration costs.

56. Choose an experienced property surveyor.

Prior to taking on a lease, have an experienced property surveyor perform a dilapidations liability assessment and prepare an accurate schedule of condition, including detailed photos of the state of the building where required.

57. Keep on top of any maintenance issues.

The easiest way to do this is to have a fixed maintenance plan in place from day one, which means you can virtually forget about it and focus your attention on the business. This also makes it much easier to budget for maintenance issues across the year.

58. Find a good dilapidations expert.

During or at the end of your lease, find a good dilapidations expert to help dispute and reduce any dilapidations claim.

59. Improve your fire protection system.

Reduce property insurance by ensuring it has a suitable fire protection system in place which is regularly maintained.

60. Reduce insurance premiums by installing a NACOSS/NSI intruder alarm.

Most insurers insist on you having this as a basic requirement to the policy and will often refuse any claim should it not be in place or without an active maintenance plan in place.

61. Install insurance approved doors, windows and locks.

Ensure doors, windows, and locks are insurance approved, and are well maintained with a maintenance plan in place.

62. Install an insurance approved safe on the premises.

Where higher value items or cash is kept on the premises, this may be a mandatory requirement from the insurance company, but where not mandatory, it should help reduce premiums, and in any case is good practice to protect the business from theft, fire and flood risk.

63. Use Insurance approved CCTV.

Install an insurance approved CCTV system which is remotely monitored and maintained by an NSI/SIA approved surveillance company.

64. Have staff checked for criminal records.

Have any key holders to the premises and any staff CRB checked and advise the insurers of this process.

Ensure that this process is clearly documented with certificates stored securely for use later if making a claim.

65. **Inspect and trim any trees or bushes regularly.**

    This has multiple benefits. It will reduce maintenance costs in picking up dead branches. Additionally, if a tree should damage the property, it will increase insurance premiums in the future, and it could also seriously damage the business operations.

    Finally, most insurers request that this be done to reduce areas of camouflage to any prospective criminals.

    Many insurance companies have started to reject cover where there is a tree located within a set distance from the premises.

66. **Inspect all water pipes/water tanks for insulation regularly.**

    Ensuring that pipework and tanks are properly insulated will avoid the risk of suffering burst pipes or burst water tanks in the event of freezing conditions. It is advisable to check the insulation at the start and the end of the winter season.

67. **Use chemical inhibitors in your heating system.**

    Using these will stop a buildup of corrosion deposits and could improve the heating system efficiency by up to 15%. It can increase boiler efficiency by around 4%-5%.

68. **Buy equipment and maintenance provision based on life cycle costs.**

    Many businesses will buy a product or service based on upfront costs, but this option can mean higher costs later on.

Many of us have purchased a piece of electrical equipment, only for it to break down 2 months outside of its warranty. The same is true in the business world.

Some things to consider are true life cycle costs, how long the warranty runs for, costs incurred during that time, what happens outside of that period, the cost of repairs, the maintenance costs for each option, and the running costs. There may be two identical options based on price, but if one costs twice as much in maintenance costs, and overall running costs, it carries a substantially higher life cycle cost.

69. Purchase a preventive maintenance plan for each service type.

Paying a little bit upfront in properly maintaining equipment now will ensure that equipment lasts longer and reduces the need for reactive maintenance or capital replacement.

Equipment has been shown to last 10 times as long, with reactive maintenance almost being completely eliminated when a preventive maintenance plan has been implemented. Although there is an upfront cost to pay, overall costs over a 10 year term can save up to 70% over that of having no preventive maintenance plan.

In addition to the direct cost savings, it is also proven to reduce downtime in a business, it can improve the brand reputation for staff and customers, it reduces management time in dealing with problems, and it can also improve cash flow without the need to make capital replacement of equipment at unexpected times.

For example, if a business had a boiler failure, it would have to close the business down until a replacement boiler was found. This replacement could mean the business having to find anything from $10,000 to $500,000 for a new replacement boiler. Add this to the lost revenue while the business isn't trading, and the cost could quite easily double. Some businesses wouldn't be able to restart after taking such a big hit to their cash flow.

An insurance claim would be worthless, too, as all insurance companies insist on having equipment properly maintained with an ongoing documented program of maintenance for the life of the equipment.

PART 3: Energy

70. Perform an energy audit of your property.

By doing an energy audit of the property, you'll identify any weakness in the energy efficiency of the premises, and prioritize areas in order to save energy.

71. Insulate tanks and pipes.

Insulating a water tank and pipework can significantly reduce energy costs. For example a normal domestic sized tank jacket costs around $15, but will save $45 per year on the energy bill.

Likewise, an investment of around $10 in pipe insulation can generate savings of around $15 per year.

72. Replace old boilers with new energy efficient boilers.

Most boilers over ten years old can operate at between 45%-85% efficiency. This means that for every 1000 units of energy that the boiler creates, it only outputs 450 units, or 45% of it, with the rest lost to inefficiencies and to the environment. Most new boilers operate at 95% efficiency or above, with the larger scale boilers operating at much closer to 100% efficiency.

73. Insulate loft areas & ceiling voids.

Around 25% of heated/cooled air is lost through uninsulated loft areas and ceiling voids.

Although many premises already have insulation in place, most should upgrade this as it is recommended that there be a minimum of 300mm insulation. Unless constructed in the last few years, the building will probably have less than 100mm.

74. Install wall insulation.

As well as loft and roof areas, heated/cooled air is also lost through walls. This can account for as much as 66% of total heat loss. Options can vary from having cavity wall insulation to internal and external insulated boards.

75. Upgrade glazed units.

Upgrade any glazing in the building to A-rated triple glazing on north facing windows, and A-rated double glazing on south facing windows.

76. Check for gaps or broken seals in glazed units.

Check windows, doors, and glazed panels for any gaps or broken seals. Checking glazed units for draughts or gaps between the glass and the frame of anything more than 1mm can help spot areas of heat loss, and taking action at these areas can reduce energy loss.

77. Keep windows closed when using either heating or cooling equipment.

Although it seems obvious, many people will open a window when they feel it's too warm while the heating system is still operating. This can especially be the case in larger buildings with more than two or three staff working there.

78. Keep doors closed when using either heating or cooling equipment.

By keeping doors closed, the conditioned air can build up within a particular space much faster. If doors are open, the heated air will dissipate into corridors and adjacent rooms, taking much longer for the desired space to be heated.

79. Install draught strips around doors.

Over time, a building's internal parts can expand and contract, according to heat and moisture levels, both pre and post installation. This is especially evident in the first two to three years. This can mean that gaps can form around doors, leaving a small space for air to pass between areas, causing a draught. Some more expensive doors have draught strips integrated into the original door. Where this isn't the case, adding a draught strip can be an inexpensive way to improve the energy efficiency of a space.

80. Install sensors to doors and windows.

Install sensors to automatically switch off heating or cooling equipment in the event of doors or windows being opened. Having these sensors linked to an alarm can also help in changing staff behaviour around improving the energy efficiency of the building.

81. Install air curtains.

Install air curtains above external doors to stop cooled/heated air from leaving the area as much as possible.

82. Build a separate lobby.

Construct a lobby area where people/vehicles enter the building, especially where activity takes place, to stop heated/cooled air escaping.

83. **Insulate the floor.**

    Around 15% of heat/cooling is lost through the floor. Insulating a floor can be a very disruptive process to your business, and so should only be considered as part of a phased or complete refurbishment of the building.

84. **Install an underfloor heating system.**

    This is the most efficient type of heating system as it's provided at feet level and travels up to the head level. It's also equally distributed across the area unlike conventional heating systems. It can be controlled by area, but is not as focused as plugging in a single electric fan heater next to an occupant.

    There are two types of underfloor heating system: firstly, a piped system, and secondly, an electric mat system.

The electric mat system is much easier to control and it has almost instantaneous heat switch on/off, but is fairly expensive on running costs. The piped system is much cheaper on running costs, using a network of pipes run around the floor area and a central heat generator which can be from biomass, gas, oil boilers, pumping heated liquid around the network of pipes until the area is up to the required temperature.

The piped system takes much longer to heat up/cool down, but this problem can be rectified by incorporating a weather watching device, along with automated timing based on occupancy levels in the building.

Using an underfloor system also means that wall areas are not taken up by radiators or ductwork.

This type of measure is only really suitable for premises with a phased or complete refurbishment, as it requires major areas of flooring to be open, but it can be tied into insulating the floor area at the same time.

85. **Turn PC's and other electrical equipment off sleep mode.**
By completely powering down equipment, a small 2-3 man office can save around $100/year.

86. **Turn your heating thermostat down by one Celsius.**
Turning down your heating thermostat by just one degree Celsius will save 8% of your heating energy consumption.

87. **Turn up your cooling thermostat by 1 Celsius.**

    Turning the thermostat up by one Celsius will save 8% of your cooling energy consumption.

88. **Automate all systems.**

    Automating the control of both heating and cooling systems to come on just before staff arrive (if needed) saves the equipment running when staff aren't in the building.

89. **Remove all human control.**

    Removing the ability for the building occupants to adjust the temperature can help you maintain an even and comfortable temperature for all occupants of the building.

For example, one occupant might feel it's too warm, and so turn the air conditioning on, while the other occupants then find it too cool and so switch on the heating.

Apart from having two systems operating against each other, it also means that both systems have to work extra hard to heat/cool the pre-treated air just to get it back to what it was already. By removing all control, it removes the ability of staff to do this.

90. **Provide staff with branded workwear sweatshirts and jackets.**

This will improve your brand presence externally, but also means that building occupants will be less inclined to turn up the heating as they'll be wearing sweatshirts and don't feel the cold as much.

By providing staff with sweatshirts, you could turn the heating down by 2 or 3 Celsius, and they won't notice it, saving you almost 25% on your heating energy bill. Doing the same for air conditioned space will achieve the same end result too.

91. Develop an energy saving culture, & ambassador program.

Provide rewards to the best individual, or group for performance. Such a scheme could be used for promoting your business environmental credentials to the outside world and go towards strengthening your brand to existing and potential customers.

92. Install blinds on windows to avoid overheating.

Installing blinds, especially on south facing windows, reduces the amount of heat entering the building, which in turn reduces the amount of cooling needed.

This is an additional form of controlling the heating/cooling of a building.

93. Use solar shading on the building.
Using solar shading on a building reflects the sun's glare away from windows, and can also improve the appearance of some buildings.

94. Turn the water temperature down.
If your business uses laundry equipment, turn the water temperature down to 30 Celsius instead of 40 Celsius.

95. Buy energy efficient appliances.
Most electrical appliances come with an energy efficiency rating between A and G. Choosing the most energy efficient may cost a little more upfront, but can save up to $130 per year in running costs.

96. Replace baths with showers.

If your business has a requirement to provide bathing facilities, such as a hotel, remove all baths and instead install showers with water efficient heads. This could save you up to $200 per year on energy and water bills per bath.

97. Replace older lighting with new LED lighting.

Replace halogen, discharge and fluorescent lighting with LED smart lighting. This can save up to 87% of running costs, it has a life expectancy up to 25 times as long, and has virtually zero maintenance cost.

98. Install daylight level sensors to control light levels.

This means that if the sun starts to shine mid-day, the lighting system will automatically dim, thus saving energy.

99. **Install occupancy sensors rather than light switches.**

This can be split up just to operate on a very small and specific area such as one desk space, within a much wider office area. It can be used for any building type rather than just office spaces.

100. **Use bright colors for decorating surfaces.**

Wherever possible, decorate brightly colored walls, floors, and ceilings using reflective materials.

101. **Reduce ceiling heights.**

If a ceiling height is above 2.4mtr high, aim to reduce it by installing a new suspended ceiling. Reducing a ceiling that is 3.5 mtr high to 2.4mtr can reduce heating, cooling and lighting demand for that area by over 30%.

102. Use reflective tape on the rear of radiators.

Using reflective tape on the back of radiators reduces heat from being lost into the wall.

103. Zone areas of the building for better control.

Dividing a floorspace into localized zones to better control the heating/cooling/lighting system means that if only a small area of the premises are used, you won't need to heat/cool/light the entire floorspace.

104. Install area thermostats for each zone.

Installing individual thermostats for each zone means that when a smaller area is at the correct temperature, the zone switches off, making the equipment much more efficient.

105. Install a buffer tank to reduce boiler cycling.

Integrating a buffer/accumulator tank for storing heated/cooled water ready for circulation into the premises reduces boiler cycling, and helps keep it running efficiently. If using a buffer tank, ensure that it is not oversized, as an oversized tank will not use all of its water capacity before the temperature of the water is lost.

106. Generate your own energy onsite.

Generate your own energy on site and sell surplus energy back to the grid. This reduces your reliance on the energy company whilst reducing your energy costs.

107. Use heat recovery to recirculate heat.

Taking heated air from one area, cleaning it, and redistributing it elsewhere in the premises can mean saving on heat generation.

108. Install Solar PV Panels.

Installing solar PV panels to generate your own electricity from the sun means you get free electricity and any excess electricity can be sold back to the grid.

109. Install a wind turbine.

Installing a wind turbine to generate electricity from the wind onsite means you can generate electricity every time the wind blows. Excess electricity can be sold back to the grid.

110. Install a CHP unit onsite.

Installing a CHP (Combined heat and power) unit to generate heat/cooling and power from either gas or biomass fuel can mean lower energy costs, and excess energy can be exported either to the grid or sold to neighboring buildings.

111. **Install a Biomass Boiler.**

Installing a biomass boiler to generate heat/cooling which uses biomass fuel such as pellets, logs or chips can significantly reduce the cost of heating your premises.

112. **Install an Air Source Heat Pump.**

Installing an air source heat pump to generate heat/cooling from the air can reduce the cost of running your heating/cooling systems.

113. **Install a Ground Source Heat Pump.**

Install a ground source heat pump to generate heat/cooling from the ground. This is done by both digging a large pit and burying coils of pipework, or by drilling a large borehole into the earth's core. This is an alternative to Air Source Heat Pumps.

114. Install solar water heating (solar thermal).

This generates hot water from the sun. It works the same way as solar PV, except that water is contained in a number of cylinders within the panel and piped to your storage cylinder.

115. Replace any electric storage heaters.

Replace electric storage heaters with an efficient boiler system. Dependent on their tariff, storage heating can be one of the most expensive types of heating systems as well as being inefficient.

116. Switch energy suppliers.

Comparing and switching energy suppliers can save over 10% on your energy bills.

117. Pay by direct debit.

Ask your energy supplier if paying by direct debit is cheaper or what the cheapest option to save money on your energy bills might be.

118. Bulk buy your energy.

Group together with others in your local area to increase buying power and get a larger discount.

119. Reduce water usage.

Reducing water usage, particularly hot water, will reduce your energy bills, both in terms of heating the water but also if the property is fixed to a water meter. This will reduce the units consumed by the property, reducing the overall water bill as well.

120. Perform a pressure test to the water supply.

Performing a pressure test on the water supply will identify any potential leaks to the system. This is especially relevant between the external meter and where the water enters the building. Even a small dribble at each connection in the pipe can amount to extra costs in your water cost over time.

121. Check the meter calibration.

Installing secondary metering to all metered services will allow you to compare your official metered supply with your own meter readings. Inaccuracies of up to 40% have been found in some premises, which could substantially save your business money.

122. Use the boiler to generate hot water.
Rather than using electric immersion heaters to heat water, use the boiler combined with a thermal store or accumulator tank.

123. Replace hand dryers with new energy efficient units.
Install energy efficient hand dryers in place of old inefficient dryers or paper towels.

124. Go digital and remove paper wastage.
Remove paper based processes from the business; instead, use IT based processes to reduce waste from the business.

125. Use occupancy sensors to reduce water.
Use sensors on taps, especially in public areas, to prevent persons leaving taps running, and toilets flushing.

126. Don't heat up the water when the building isn't occupied.

Savings can be achieved by installing either an automated control system or taking very basic steps such as installing a time clock.

127. Fit flow regulators to showers to reduce water.

Though this shouldn't be performed on electric showers, a flow regulator will reduce the amount of water being used.

128. Replace electric shower units to conventional mixer shower units.

By replacing electric shower units with mixer units, it means that an efficient boiler system can generate the heat rather than using a high rated electric shower unit to generate it.

An electric shower can use up to 40 times as much energy to heat the water, over that of a boiler generating heated water at much greater efficiency and scale.

129. Buy Waterwise recommended products.

Only buy water efficiency products that have been labeled by the Waterwise recommended checkmark.

130. Educate staff.

Educate staff and customers on the best way to be energy and water efficient. By educating them on how best to use energy, they can take what they've learnt, and use it in their home environment too, meaning it starts to become a habit and way of life for them, thus cementing the process in their mind.

131. Repair dripping taps as quickly as possible.

A dripping tap can waste 5,500 liters of water in a year. Replacing a tap washer takes just a few minutes. Is it worth the effort to save so much water?

132. Fill fridges and freezers up.

Where you have empty space, use crumpled newspaper or sealed plastic containers to fill the air gap. The less space available means less space has to be cooled.

133. Clean fridge and freezer door seals.

Regularly cleaning fridge and freezer door seals, and checking that they are not ripped or missing means a fridge or freezer unit doesn't have to work harder than it needs to.

134. Keep refrigerated liquids covered.

By sealing or covering any liquids in the fridge or freezer, the unit doesn't have to work as hard. Vapors given off by the liquid make the unit work harder to cool the space.

135. Operate the refrigerated units at their optimum temperature.

Ensuring the units run at their optimum temperature can help save money in running costs, as they don't have to work harder than they need to. The optimum fridge temperature is between 3 and 5 Celsius (37 - 41 fahrenheit). For a freezer, this is minus 18 Celsius (-0.4 fahrenheit).

136. Fit automatic door closers to fridge and freezer doors.

Fitting an automatic door closer and/or an alarm system to the door will automatically close or will sound a buzzer to alert staff that the door has been left open.

137. Only place cool food in the fridge.

Letting food cool before placing it in the fridge means the fridge unit will not have to work as hard to cool the food. Hot food can cause the whole area to heat up. This is subject to hygiene precautions.

138. Properly maintain your fridge / freezer units.

A well maintained fridge/freezer unit can reduce energy consumption of the units by 30%.

139. Reduce room temperatures by fitting LED lighting.

Fit LED lighting to reduce temperatures and the need for cooling. Many traditional types of lighting create large amounts of heat, so much so that it's impossible to touch one of these units without suffering burns to the skin. An LED light unit does not create any heat whilst operating.

140. Reduce room temperatures by removing IT equipment.

Get rid of IT equipment such as servers and desktop drives from an area to reduce cooling requirements.

141. Remove phone chargers from use.

Unplug phone chargers and other transformers such as power packs when not in use.

142. Reduce unnecessary boiling.

Only boil the water that's needed when making hot drinks. One example of this can be to replace large water boilers and electric urns with localized kettles in canteen areas.

143. Close blinds at night.

Close blinds at night to keep any built up heat during the day from escaping during the colder months. It also improves security on the building.

144. Upgrade old equipment.

Upgrade and replace any energy consuming equipment that is over 10 years old, as energy efficiency reduces over time, or equipment just takes more time to achieve the same output, hence consuming more energy to achieve the same result.

145. Regularly clean windows.

Clean windows and roof lights regularly to increase natural daylight entering the building and reducing the necessary lighting.

146. Remove signage from windows.

Remove any signage or decoration from windows and doors to increase natural daylight entering the building.

147. Clean lighting diffusers, reflectors, and shades.

Cleaning diffusers, reflectors and shades helps increase light output from each unit.

148. Install horizontal blinds.

Use horizontal blinds that tilt light to the ceiling rather than using black out blinds. By reflecting light toward a white reflective ceiling, this naturally acts like an additional source of light in the room.

149. Install programmable controllers.

Fit seven day programmable controllers to any mechanical ventilation fans to prevent operation when the building isn't occupied.

150. Reset frost thermostats.

Reset any frost protection thermostats to ensure that they are not set too high.

151. Don't simultaneously use heating and cooling equipment.

This can be done by installing a management system which will isolate one unit over another.

Ideally both systems wouldn't be able to operate within the same period, for example, not operating within the same 12 hours unless for emergency operation.

152. Keep vehicle access doors closed as much as possible.

Installing alarms fitted to access doors acts as a deterrent for staff to open them, and to close them soon after.

153. Switch immersion heaters off if the boiler is running.

An immersion heater can consume 16 times as much energy to heat water over that of using a boiler. Most people do not realize that an immersion heater is switched on, and heating the water, when a boiler has already pre-heated it.

154. **Reduce excessive storage of heated water in low demand.**
If an accumulator storage tank is being used, ensure that it isn't oversized, as it will not be able to use all of the heat generated. Consequently, it will have been heated up for no reason.

155. **Fit circulatory fans to improve air circulation.**
Fit circulatory fans in high ceiling and high bay areas (for example, in a warehouse environment) to stop heat from collecting in high level pockets of the roof space.

156. **Implement regular service maintenance for heating equipment.**
Having a regular service plan on heating equipment can save over 10% on heating costs.

157. Install boiler sequencing.

If using multiple boilers, install boiler sequencing controls.

158. Replace old boiler equipment.

If boilers are over 10 years old, consider replacing them for more efficient boilers. When considering an alternative replacement boiler, the total lifecycle cost of each option should be considered, including maintenance costs, likely fuel costs in the future, life expectancy, capital cost, etc

159. Adjust time clock settings.

Check that boiler time clock settings are correct or adjust if necessary to prevent operating out of hours. Many times a staff member, rather than checking the time clock is set correctly will simply just 'advance' the boiler so that it fires in manual mode. This means the boiler could wind up operating 24 hours a day

160. Use occupancy sensors for extract fans.

Install time controls with occupancy sensors on local extract fans.

161. Clean any fan grilles and ductwork to ensure it operates efficiently.

It's a mandatory requirement that ductwork is cleaned internally on a regular basis, but many don't realize that it can improve suction which also improves the efficiency of the system as it doesn't have to work for as long to extract the same volume of air.

162. Use immersion heaters only in emergency situations.

Switching off immersion heaters can prevent accidental use when the boiler is already heating water.

163. Control outside lighting better.
Fit time controls, combined with photocell sensors, to control outside lighting.

164. Replace old fan units with new.
Replace any old inefficient fan units with high efficiency units, incorporating variable speed drives where appropriate.

165. Remove warm air with the ventilation system.
Rather than using air conditioning to cool a building, use the ventilation system to remove warm air at night, which reduces demand for air conditioning the following day.

166. Stop operating Air conditioning units under 24 Celsius.

Adjust temperature set points so that air conditioning does not operate under 24 Celsius (75 fahrenheit) unless for a specific process requirement.

167. Increase air circulation.

Increase air recirculation when using air conditioning to reduce demand on the system.

168. Use solar film to reduce heat.

Use solar film on south facing windows to reduce overheating in the summer and reduce demand on air conditioning.

169. Use natural ventilation to cool a building.

Use natural cross ventilation to cool a building rather than air conditioning.

170. Use door closers to separate areas.

Fit automatic door closers to separate spaces where air conditioning/heating is being used within that area and to prevent treated air escaping to other areas.

171. Perform preventive maintenance to air conditioning equipment.

Preventive maintenance reduces downtime, can reduce costs by up to 30%, and improves the life expectancy of equipment.

172. Replace older motors and drives with high efficiency units.

Old motors can be very inefficient. As they get older, inefficiencies are increased, and it costs more to run them. Replace these with new high efficiency units.

173. Perform thermal imaging on equipment.

Perform thermal imaging inspections on equipment to assess how hard they are working. Assess the reasons why those pieces of equipment are working harder than others, and rectify where possible.

Upgrade any identified equipment that cannot be rectified. Often older equipment will have to work harder to generate the same level of output, which means it uses more energy to create that output.

174. Remove all unused equipment.

Remove/isolate any equipment that is no longer doing a useful job.

175. Replace oversized motors.

Replace oversized motors with correct sized high efficiency motors. Some motors have been previously installed as an oversized unit, in the false belief that if it didn't have to work as hard, it would use less energy. With the latest high efficiency motors, motors can be sized for the load they are driving, and still use much less energy than their older alternatives.

176. Replace worn drive belts and pulleys on motors.

Motors that work harder use more energy to do the same job.

177. Install voltage optimization units.

Consider installing voltage optimization units to improve motor performance as the electricity supplied to the motor is kept constant meaning the motor doesn't have to work harder as it fluctuates.

178. Properly maintain electric motors and drives.

Properly maintaining electric motors and drives means less down time, and more efficient running. Putting in place a preventive maintenance plan is a good way to achieve this.

179. Install variable speed drives.

Replace fixed speed motors with variable speed drives, especially for fans, pumps, and air compressors.

180. Install building controls.

This can save up to 20% on energy costs, and improve how the building operates.

181. Regularly check time clocks.
Check that all time clocks are set at the correct time and day. Making a quick check of these weekly can help you save considerably.

182. Set the correct on/off cycles.
Check that all time clocks have correct on/off cycles set.

183. Regularly check all thermostats.
Check that all thermostats are set to the correct setting and adjust if necessary.

184. Check occupancy sensors are set up correctly.
If occupancy sensors are installed, check their sensitivity and run time, and adjust where necessary.

185. Install occupancy sensors for all services.

If an occupancy sensor isn't already fitted to control a piece of equipment, consider whether fitting one could reduce the time that equipment operates.

For example, if a piece of equipment only needs to operate when someone is present, then fitting an occupancy sensor to that piece of equipment will save money.

186. Encourage staff to suggest ways of reducing energy.

Tying this into some form of reward scheme can help build habits for your workforce, and a company mission around sustainability.

187.   Fit timers to electrical appliances.

Fit seven day timers to all equipment, such as vending machines, where they are left on normally, so that these can be isolated when the building isn't occupied.

188.   Use the built in energy saving function.

If equipment has a built in energy saving function, set this up to operate

189.   Swap separate devices for multifunction devices.

Use multifunction devices instead of separate devices such as individual printers and copiers; use a central multi-function, multi user device.

Whilst the energy efficiency will be increased with a central unit, it should also be cheaper when replacing ink cartridges.

190. Install flat screen monitors and TV's.

Replace old monitors and TV's with new flat screen models.

191. Switch to portable IT equipment.

Where possible, use laptop or tablet PCs instead of desktops. These save 90% energy over desktops.

192. Reduce overcooling a refrigerated space.

Do not overcool refrigeration equipment. Every 1 Celsius equates to 2% of energy consumption on an efficient system, but more on an older inefficient system.

193. Clean refrigerated display cabinets.

Regularly clean refrigerated display cabinets. Doing this removes buildup of deposits over vents and thermostats, and the equipment can continue to operate efficiently.

194. Use night blinds on refrigerated cabinets.

Use well fitted night blinds or covers on all open cabinets to reduce cooling load during non-trading hours.

195. Use a glass riser on refrigerated cabinets.

Use a glass riser (weir plate) at the front of display cabinets to save approx. 3% on energy costs for running each cabinet.

196. Inspect refrigerated pipework regularly.

Check the condition of any refrigerated pipework insulation and replace if necessary.

197. Use chiller sequencing to control multi chillers.

Optimize chiller sequencing to share refrigeration demand if multiple chillers are present.

198. Plan preventive maintenance tasks for refrigeration.

Have a suitable preventive maintenance plan for refrigeration equipment. This can remove downtime along with loss of perishable goods lost during the downtime of a poorly maintained refrigeration unit.

199. **Assess where heat is escaping from the building.**

Perform a thermal imaging assessment to the external facades of a building to determine where heat may be escaping.

200. **Repair identified gaps in the building fabric.**

Fill or repair any gaps in walls to prevent treated air from escaping.

201. **Remove damp before upgrading insulation.**

Rectify any areas of dampness in the building before replacing affected insulation.

202. Use docking seals for unloading vehicles.

Where vehicles are unloaded at bays within a building, use docking seals around the doors.

203. Replace compressed air tools with electric.

Where compressed air tools are used, consider if electric tools can be used instead. Air tools cost 10 times as much in energy to run.

204. Properly maintain compressed air equipment.

Have an active preventive maintenance plan for compressed air tools and equipment.

205. Repair airline leaks

Repair any leaks in the airlines as soon as possible. Every bit of air that escapes from the airline has to be replaced by the compressor. If the air isn't used for its purpose, then it's a waste of energy.

206. Use the coldest air source possible for the compressor input.

If positioned externally, position the air compressor to the north face of the area or building with shading to the south, east and west sides. Reducing the air input temperature by 6 Celsius can reduce energy consumption by 2%.

207. Remove unused lines.

Remove any old or unused air lines or outlets to reduce the volume of air required in the airline system.

208. Separate compressed air network into zones.

Fit zone isolation valves to areas of the airline circuits to reduce the compressed air requirement. The longer the airline network, the larger the demand for compressed air to fill it.

209. Combine demand for heat with other local properties.

By grouping together with other local properties, you can achieve much greater efficiencies both in boiler efficiency and capital cost. By installing a centralized boiler plant and distributing metered heat to each property, each participant pays only for the heat used.

210. Group your energy management with other local businesses.

By grouping together the energy management function, the process can be performed more efficiently, which saves money for all parties.

211. Group your demand for sustainability with other local businesses.

Every business needs to improve its sustainability practices. Working together with other local businesses reduces duplication, and costs in doing so can be divided across many businesses, while each still gains the benefit.

Conclusion

It was our aim to give you an insight into how you could reduce the costs of operating your real estate. We do not expect that you'll be able to do most of this work yourself, and we encourage you to consult a professional with relevant experience to create a list of viable opportunities, along with any payback where an upfront investment is needed.

It's also important to prioritize opportunities according to both budget, and also those opportunities with the greatest impact, or shortest payback period.

About the Author

Wayne Fox is a business re-ignitor, industry disruptor, commercial property developer, futurist, best-selling Author, & investor. Director of the Enyaw group, a UK-based investment firm that invests in *'freedom lifestyle'* ventures. He is experienced in achieving 7 & 8-figure revenue growth across previous SME ventures.

My online links:

Wayne Fox Website: www.wayne-fox.co.uk

Enyaw Group: www.enyawgroup.com

Enyaw Capital: www.enyawcapital.com

Enyaw Property: www.enyawproperty.co.uk

Linkedin:https://www.linkedin.com/in/waynefoxuk

Twitter: https://twitter.com/WayneFoxUK1

Instagram:https://www.instagram.com/waynefoxuk

Youtube:https://www.youtube.com/@WayneFoxUK

Udemy:https://www.udemy.com/user/wayne-fox-6

www.ingramcontent.com/pod-product-compliance
Lightning Source LLC
Chambersburg PA
CBHW070303230526
45470CB00002B/705